Old St. Nick Carving
Classic Santas from Wood

David Sabol

Text written with
& photography by
Jeffrey B. Snyder

Schiffer Publishing Ltd

77 Lower Valley Road, Atglen, PA 19310

Dedication

I dedicate this book to my children — Kyle, 5 1/2 years
old and Jessie, 20 months, which are very precious ages.
You fill my life with joy and make me laugh.
Follow your dreams, I did and I'm glad. I love you both.

— Dad

Contents

Library of Congress Cataloging-in-Publication Data

Sabol, David.
    Old St. Nick Carving: classic santas from wood/David
Sabol: text written with and photography by Jeffrey B. Snyder.
      p. cm.
    ISBN 0-7643-0039-3 (paper)
    1. Wood-carving--Patterns. 2. Wood-carved figurines.
3. Santa Claus in art. I. Snyder, Jeffrey B. II. Title.
TT199.7.S2117 1996
736'.4--dc20   96-13539
              CIP

Printed in China

ISBN: 0-7643-0039-3

Published by Schiffer Publishing, Ltd.
77 Lower Valley Road
Atglen, PA 19310
Please write for a free catalog.
This book may be purchased from the publisher.
Please include $2.95 postage.
Try your bookstore first.

We are interested in hearing from authors
with book ideas on related subjects.

Introduction

This highly animated Santa — like the old man and the sea — is bound for places unknown. Adventure and thrills are what keep the child in all of us alive. This whimsical, expressive, adventuresome St. Nick keeps that child thriving and is a joy to add to any Santa collection.

This project is carved from an unseasoned (green) block of white pine and painted with oil stains. As a special gift for all seasons, I'll give you a few hints: 1) about pine block carving — keep the block moist and your carving will be much easier, 2) with a change of color, the brown trout may become a rainbow or a brook trout, and 3) if you make a few alterations, Santa will be riding on a bass, sailfish, or the black marlin from The Old Man and the Sea.

Each step of this project will be clearly described with simple, easily followed directions and illustrated with color photographs. Patterns and galley photographs for a variety of Santas, with different outfits and preoccupations, have been provided to spark your imagination. Even the venerable Mrs. Claus makes an appearance with a pastry to keep her husband fit for his Christmas rounds.

The tools I have chosen for this project are: a power arm (to hold the work in progress, freeing both hands for carving), a band saw (for cutting out the figure's basic shape from a pine block), a bench knife (I use a Warren #B11 that has been reshaped — the knife blade has been beveled to a point for fine detail), gouges (numbers 7, 8, 9, 11, and 15), a #7 fishtail gouge, V tools (numbers 12 and 15), veiners (a small veiner and a #12), and a wood burner. Power tools are never used after the initial blank is cut from the pine block.

We will be working with these tools on the whole carving as a single sculpture. We will not finish one part first and then move on to the next. This method, working on the entire piece together, will keep all of the forms in perspective and in relationship to each other.

Oil stains are created by mixing oil paints with Minwax Natural on freezer paper. These stains are applied with brushes (a Langnickel fan brush and brushes numbers 1, 4 and 8). I use a Grumbacker #8 as my main brush along with a Grumbacker #4 and Langnickel #1. The colorful stains help give my Santas a vibrant, individual character.

Pattern reduced to 58% of original size.

Carving Santa and the Trout

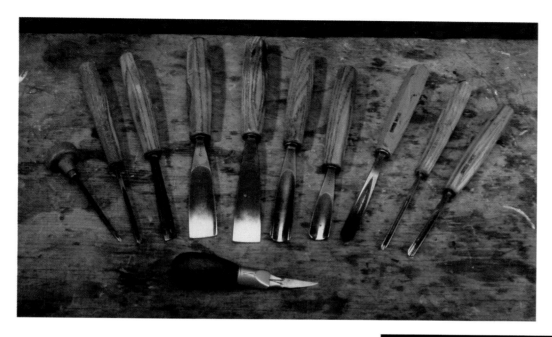

Here are the carving hand tools you will need for this project. They are (from left to right): a small palm gouge, #12 V tool (small [4mm] and large [10mm]), #3 - 25mm gouge, #2 - 25mm gouge, #8 - 18mm gouge, #7 - 14mm gouge, a bent #12 - 10mm V tool, #11 - 2mm gouge, and a #9 - 5mm gouge. All of these chisels are Swiss made. The bench knife in front has a 11B blade which has been reshaped — changing the bevel, profile, and sweep to ensure that the blade comes to a very fine point.

This block was taken right from a log, blocked out with a chain saw, and the profile was cut out with a band saw. The block measures 4 1/2" x 8" x 10". The vertically running wide grain is more suitable for carving than a narrow grain. This piece may also be laminated together from smaller boards.

The roughed out pine block is fastened to a power arm with screws. The power arm is a hydraulic piston on a swivel ball. It allows the carver to use both hands for carving and manipulating the work with ease. When the piece is in a position that satisfies you, the arm may be locked. Once it is fastened to the power arm, draw in a center line along the pine block.

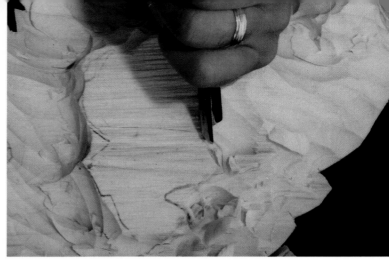

Draw in the outline of the Santa. Using the #8 gouge, we are going to start by defining where the Santa figure and the fish will be. Establish the location of the fish under Santa's body. Keep in mind that the fish's body will be curved to one side. For the moment we are leaving the head and tail alone.

Carving in the top of the right knee.

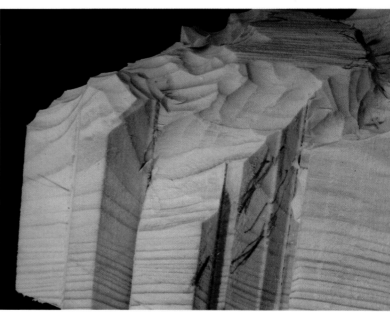

Begin to define the creel on Santa's back that will hold a smaller fish, already caught.

Establish the angle of the creel across Santa's back.

Carve in Santa's hat tassel where it falls down in back. This is just a small ball shape.

Raise Santa's left leg for more animation in the pose.

We're giving the tail and head a semi-circular curve away from the left side.

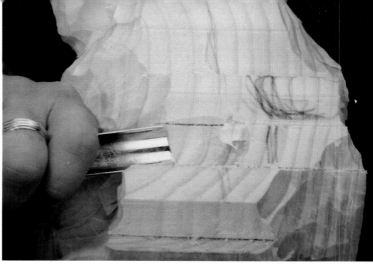

Here is the general outline of the raise left boot and the two hands holding the rod. Remove excess stock away from the left boot, establishing the location of the stomach.

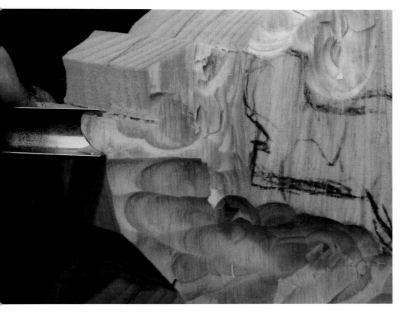

Add some curve to the head as well. Work in toward the center line.

Establishing the right shoulder under the ball of the hat.

Establishing the location of the head. Working in toward the center line again.

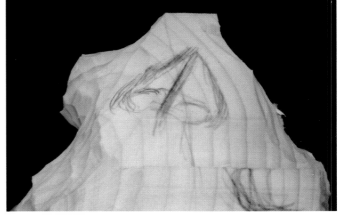

The head is going to be on at a slight angle. I have drawn in where the cheeks and the hood are going to be. The center line of the face is on an angle from the original center line of the head. This way we get a turned face.

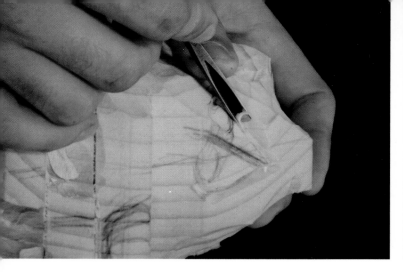

Using a number 15 V gouge, cut in the line of the hat and cheeks.

Draw in the cheeks.

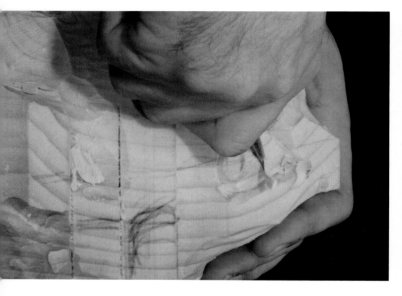

Begin to recess the forehead back into the hood with a bench knife. Make sure not to cut back too deeply toward the back of the hood or you Santa will appear to be missing the back of his head.

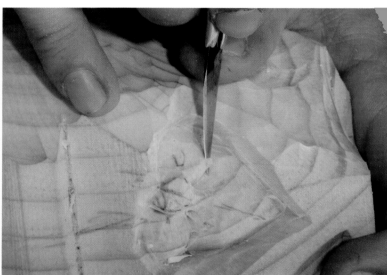

Rounding the cheeks on either side of the nose.

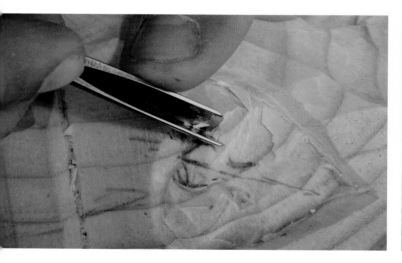

Draw in the location of the nose. Using the #15 V tool, recess around the nose.

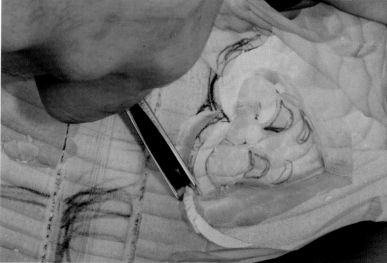

Rounded cheeks and nose. Draw in the rest of the face for reference. Take the #15 V tool and cut deeply along the lines of the mustache.

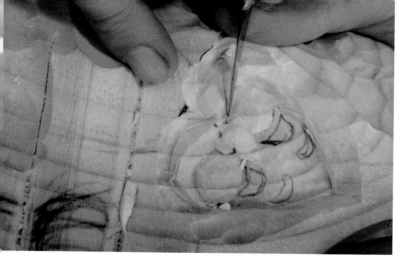

Establish the nostrils, the bottom of the nose, and the shape of the mustache, both on the top and bottom.

Using a large V tool, make a few large cuts along these lines. We are carving all around the piece like this to keep the proportions in check, to keep from ending up with a head that is too large or too small.

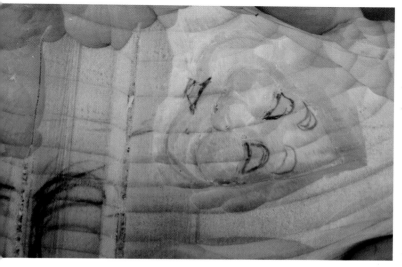

Draw in the mouth again.

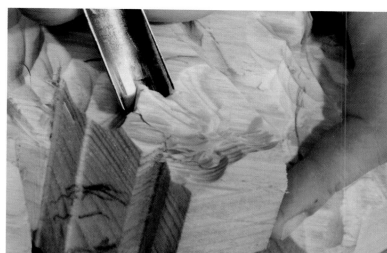

Using a #8 gouge, cut away the excess wood around the curved and draped tail that extends out of the top of the creel. The creel itself is shown penciled in on the lower right hand side of the photograph. Remember, the creel runs down Santa's back on a diagonal. The #8 gouge is good for removing a lot of wood while remaining in control.

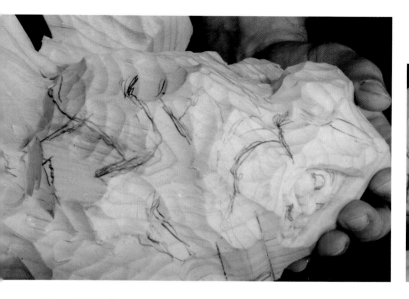

Draw in the lines where the leg, rump, beard, and fur ruff around the hat should be located.

Rounding down the body, here I am rounding Santa's ample middle and his knee.

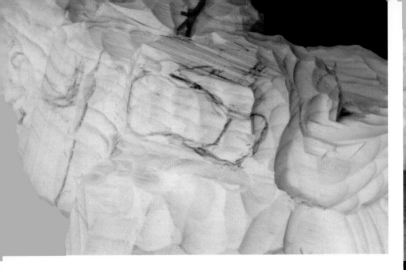

Cut away the excess stock from in front of the upraised left foot.

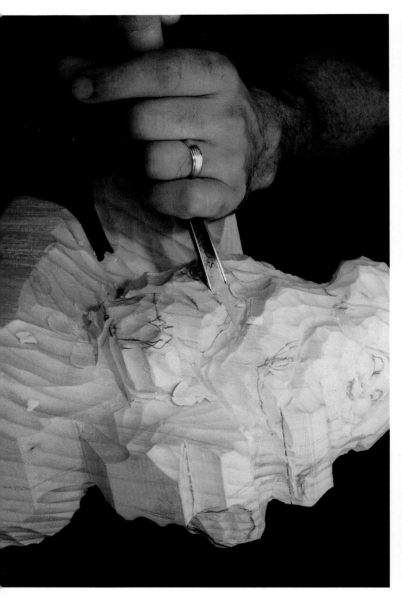

Rounding the right-hand side with a #15 V gouge. You can see the fish's head taking shape along with Santa's side and legs. The curve of the tail is also visible.

Rounding the creel. While you are here, make sure the cheeks on Santa's behind are both on the same plane while you are rounding. One cheek far ahead of the other would look awkward and give the impression that the fish was coming through Santa rather than of him riding on top of the fish.

Using the #3 gouge, recess the top of the creel to expose the trout's tail.

Outline the beard and cut it in with a #12 V tool. This will also help define the belly.

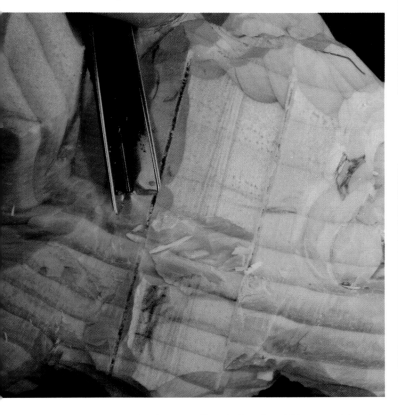

Here is the separation between Santa's beard and his cupped hands. The hands are off to the sides, holding the fishing rod. I am using the #12 V tool to separate the hands from the beard.

We're carving a green piece of wood. When it gets a little dry, spray it with water. This gives the wood a better pliability and a cleaner cut. The water also lubricates the tool as it goes through the wood.

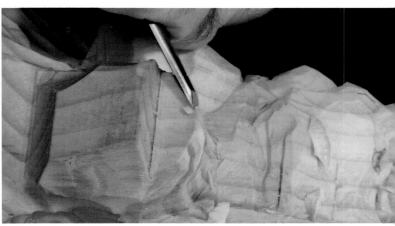

The time has come to start working on the big fish. Begin by working on the head of the fish, which is slightly turned to the right. Round down the shape of the head with a #3 gouge. The nose should come down to an almost rounded point.

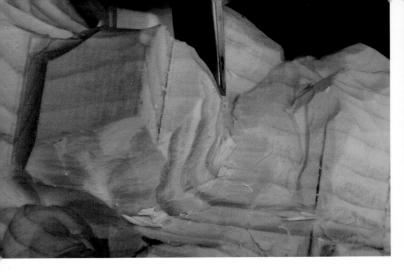

Reduce the back until Santa is sitting on the back rather than having the back coming through Santa's middle.

When the gouge won't reach, use a bench knife to continue opening the mouth.

Draw in the fish's mouth.

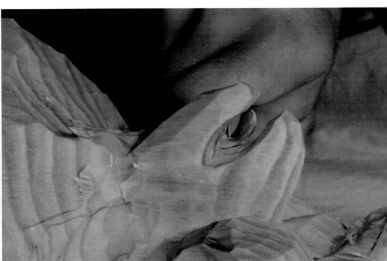

Remove some of the excess from beneath the lower jaw. Start to give the trout's lower jaw its characteristic hook shape. Draw in the fins as well.

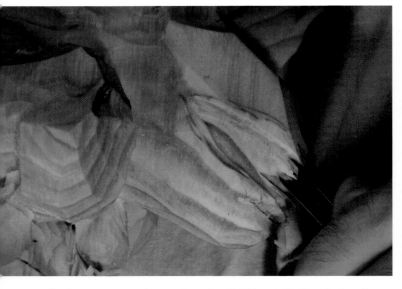

Begin to carve out the mouth with a #15 V tool. Outline the jaw lines and then take out the excess wood in the middle.

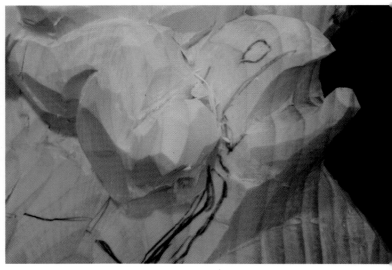

Draw in the eyes, lip line, and gills to accompany the fins.

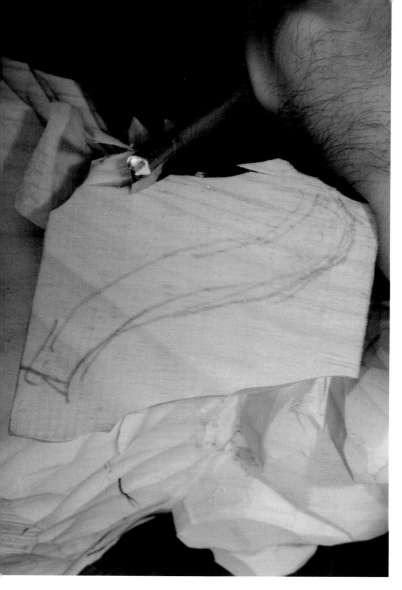

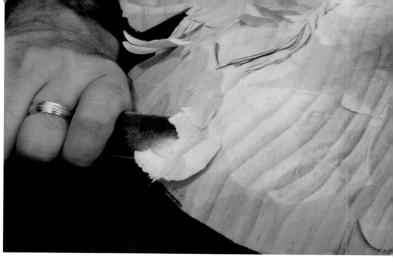

Rounding down the base with the #3 gouge. We will be carving in the fins soon.

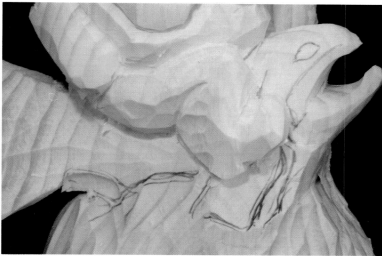

Reduce the tail with the #8 gouge. Follow the S curve guide at the base of the tail.

Draw in the rest of the fish. The pencil line at the base defines where the fish meets the water. Note the small, rear ventral fin near the underside of the tail.

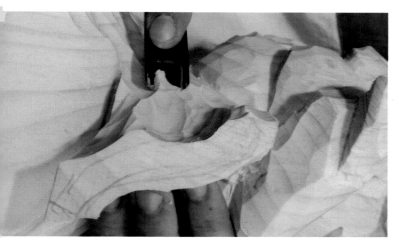

The excess stock is removed from the tail. Leave the tail thick for now to prevent it from cracking off while you are still removing large amounts of wood. All the major rounding should be done before you begin to carve in any fine details.

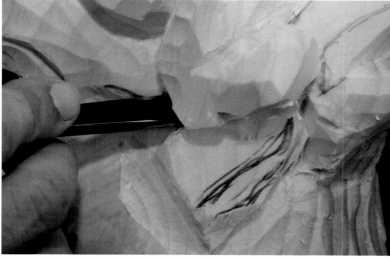

Using a #12 V tool, outline the pectoral fin.

Santa and the trout are roughed in. We are ready to start carving in the details.

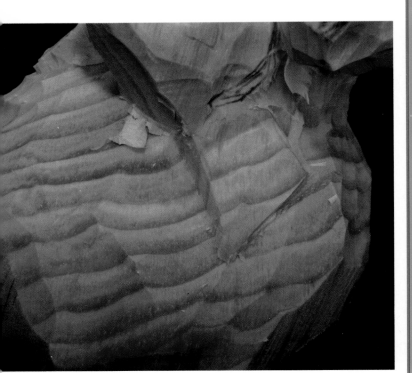

Use the #3 gouge to reduce the base up to the V cuts along the pectoral fin.

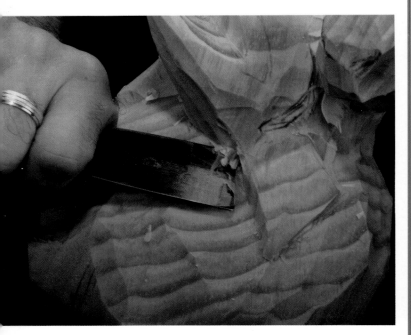

Remove excess wood from the base around the trout's neck with the #3 gouge.

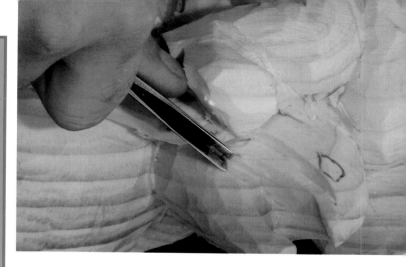

First we are going to carve in the trout's lips and gills. Use the #15 V tool to make fairly deep cuts around the upper lip. Make sure the lips are symmetrical or your fish will have a lopsided face.

The carved lip on the left side of the face.

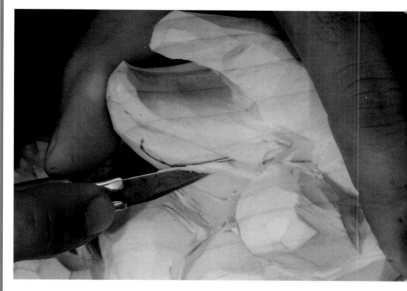

Using the bench knife, round off the sharp edge of the upper lip, blending it into the body of the trout.

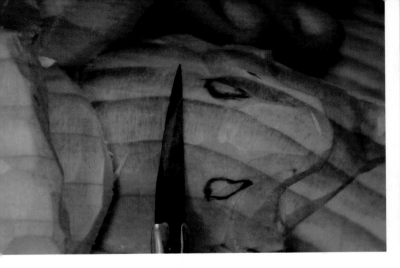

Draw the eyes in again. Make sure the eyes are on the same lines, that they are parallel, and that they are the same size. This is essential if the face is to look right.

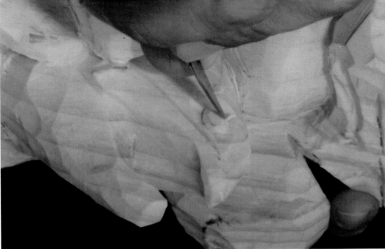

Round off the eyes until they just protrude a little beyond the sides of the head.

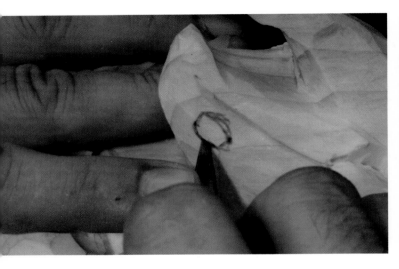

Cutting straight in with the bench knife, follow the pencil lines for the eyes. Cut deeply so you don't have to go back and try to cut them again.

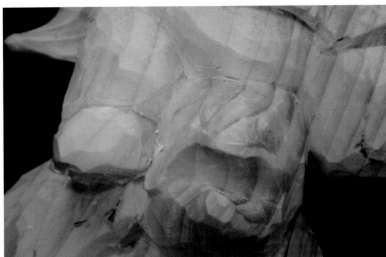

The rounded eyes.

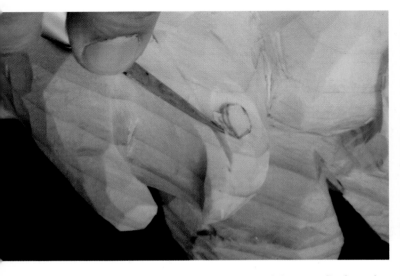

Cut away the wood from the outside edges of the eyes. Cut in to the stop cuts, leaving the eyes as two raised mounds.

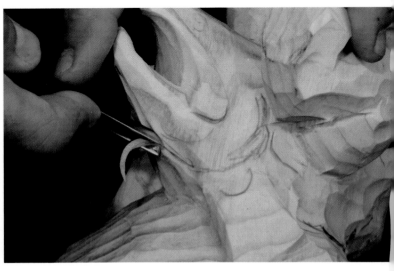

Follow the lines for the gill from the underside of the jaw all the way around with the #15 V gouge. Make two deep cuts along the gills. This will give the impression that the gills are flaring.

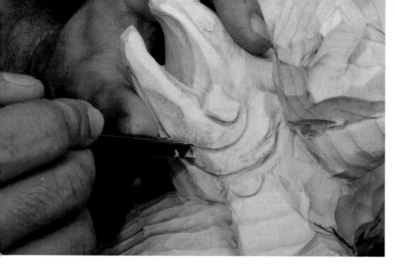

Still using the #15 V gouge, cut in the gill coverings (or plates).

Make sure that the jaw attachments remain symmetrical as you hollow out the mouth's interior.

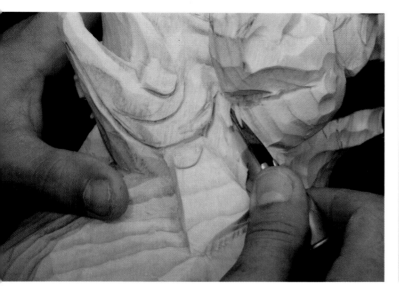

Cut under the gills on both sides of the body with the bench knife. This leaves the gills sticking out farther from the body, giving them a flared look. This gets a little tricky on the right side, Santa's boot covers part of that gill.

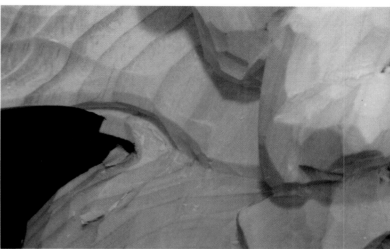

Using a small V tool, cut in for the hind fin; also cut in along the base of the body where it meets the water.

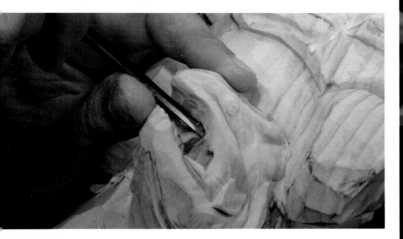

Using a #9 gouge, begin to hollow out the mouth, starting with the roof of the mouth. You only need to cut in about 1/4" to 1/2" to give the illusion of depth to the inside of the mouth.

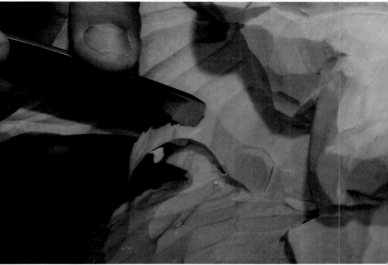

Thin down the body with a #3 gouge.

Using the bench knife, separate the upraised boot on the left from both the side of the fish and from Santa himself. Doing this will give the boot more animation.

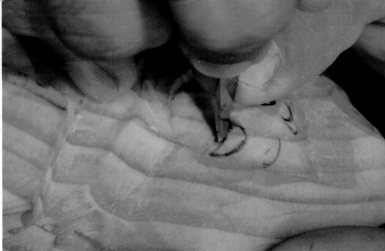

Using the bench knife, follow the pencil outline of the eyes. Make sure the bench knife is cutting straight in.

Add bends to the toe of the boot with small circular cuts of the bench knife. This creates a hollow in the center of the boot.

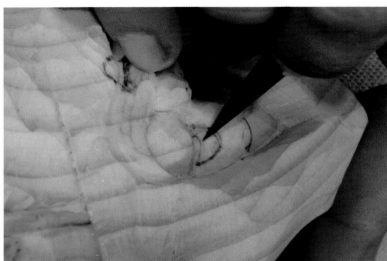

Using the very tip of the knife, round the insides of the eyeball to meet the stop cuts you have made.

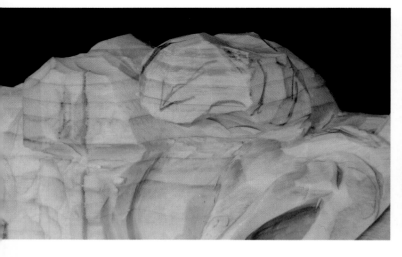

Using the bench knife, carve the boot in toward the center at the top and cut in the arch to indicate this is the left foot. Follow the penciled arrow.

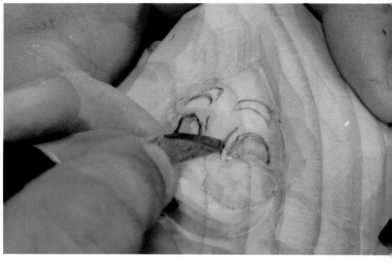

Make a stop cut along these pencil lines.

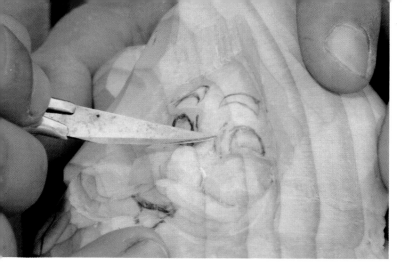

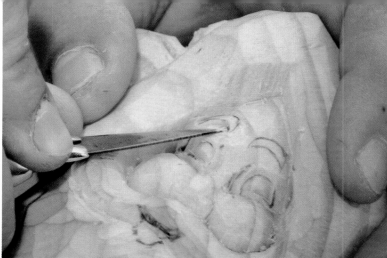

Make a little V cut up to the stop cut lines you have just created. This will produce the eyelids along the bridge of the nose.

Now recess around the forehead, leaving the eyebrow mounds raised.

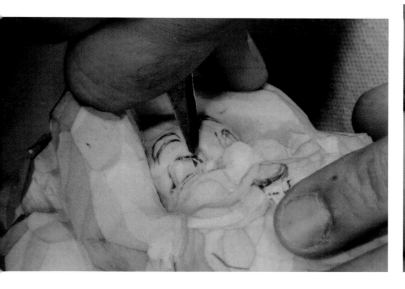

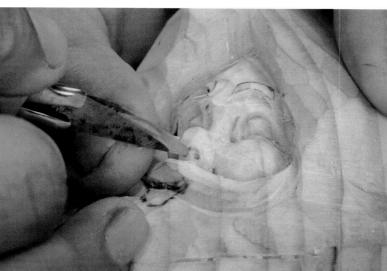

Trim the sharp corner off of the upper eyelid to soften up the transition between the eye and the forehead.

Draw in the nostrils. Using just the knife tip, which must be very sharp to cut properly, make shallow cuts — straight in. The knife blade must be very sharp, especially around the tip, to make sure features are cut in and not torn or crumbled by the knife. Most of the features are cut in just with the tip itself.

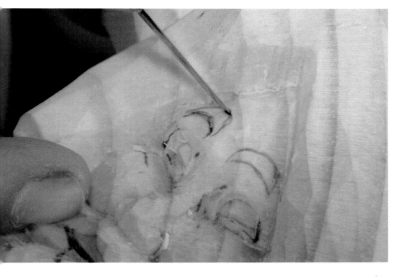

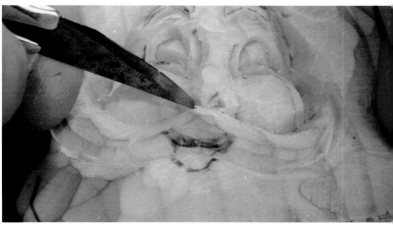

Make two little half moon cuts for the eyebrows, using the bench knife and once again cutting straight in.

Once you have cut in, just spin the blade to make a tiny semi-circular cut. The center wood should fall away.

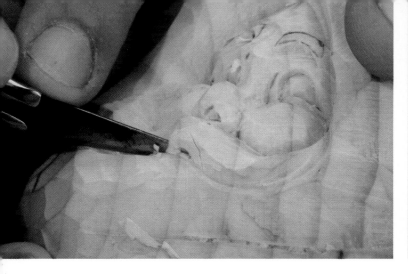

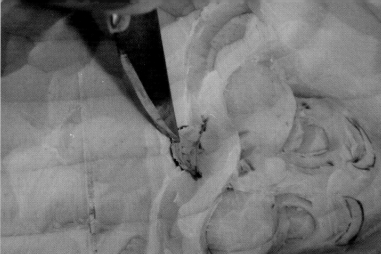

Make a small inverted V cut where the two sides of the mustache meet. The point of the V is centered under the nose.

Once you have cut around the mouth, use the blade tip to pop out the chip from the center of the mouth itself.

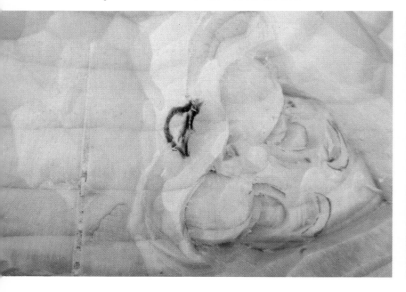

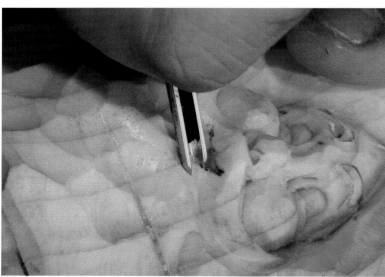

Undercut from the beard up to the V shaped stop cut of the mustache and remove a small chip of wood, separating the mustache and leaving an opening for the mouth. Draw in the mouth.

Using the #11 gouge, follow along below the lower pencil line of the mouth to give Santa a lower lip.

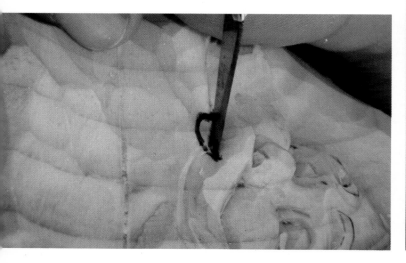

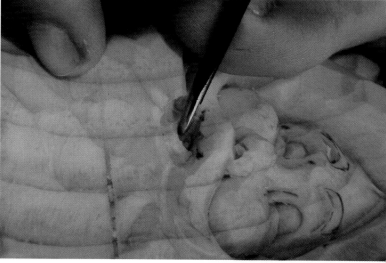

With the tip of the knife, follow the mouth lines, cutting straight in fairly deep.

A 1/16" palm gouge is very useful for cleaning out the inside of the mouth.

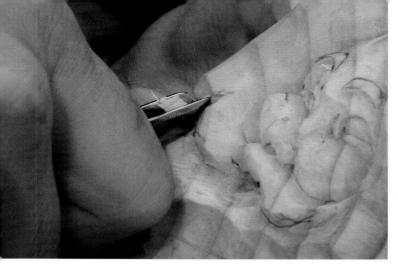

The #15 V gouge works very well when curling the ends of Santa's mustache. Pencil in guide lines and follow along below them with the gouge.

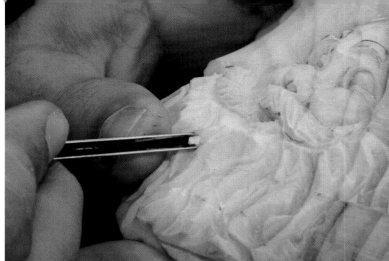

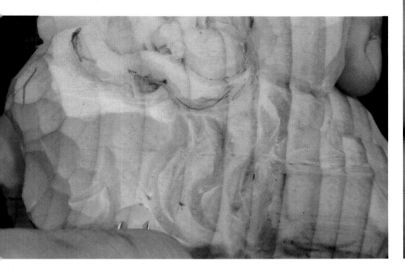

We want to give the beard a lot of life, using the #15 V gouge to create large curving and twisting large cuts. This will give the beard a whipped up look. These are deep directional cuts, have fun with them. Put in a lot of variety. However, remember to leave a mound under the mouth with no deep cuts or Santa will not have a chin.

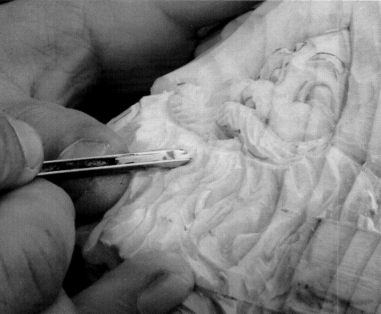

Make small cuts with the #12 V tool into the beard as well, following the larger cuts as your guides. This adds texture to the beard, adding all the little flips and curls of the beard hair. Don't go in any one direction with the beard for too long or it will look contrived. We don't want a neat beard or a "raked" effect.

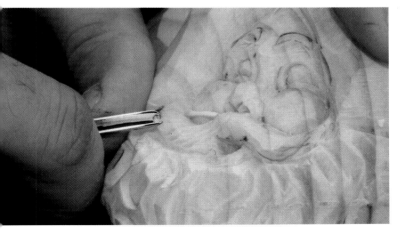

Using a small #12 V tool, make small curled cuts for the mustache. We don't want any straight cuts on the beard or mustache.

Don't forget to texture the underside of the beard as well.

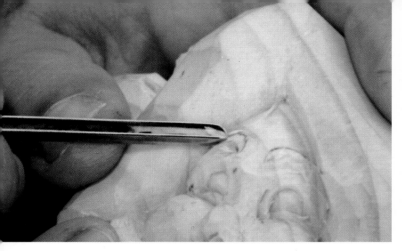

Using the #12 gouge, make small curved cuts for the eyebrows.

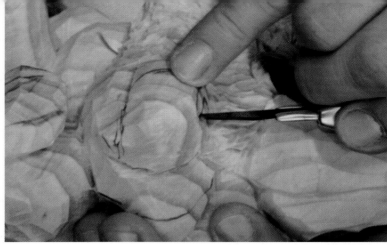

Cut straight down along the pencil lines, establishing stop cut lines around the mitten.

Now we'll move on to the hands, which are both grasping the fishing pole. They are in mittens, which make them much easier to carve. First draw in the mittens.

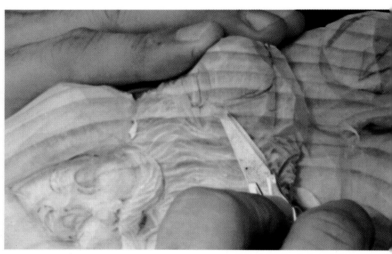

Carve up to the cut lines of the left mitten, showing that the left mitten is overlapping the right. The right mitten is recessed in this way.

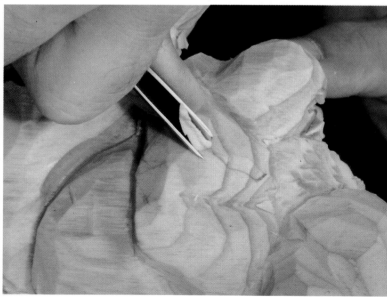

Add cuffs to the sleeve with a small V tool.

The sleeve is cut.

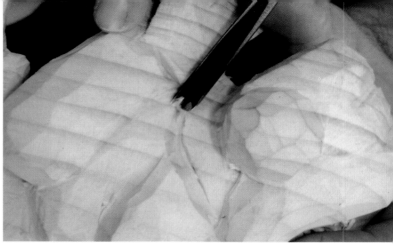

Follow the collar line with the #15 V tool to create the edge of the collar.

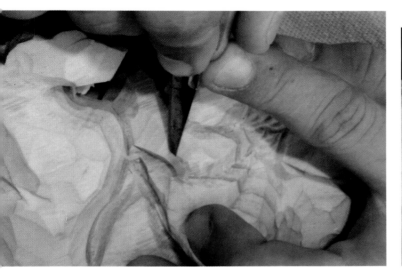

The cuff should be soft in appearance. Cut off the sharp edges along the cuff with your bench knife.

With the bench knife or chisel, make a curved cut along the collar up to the neck line. This is an upward sweep to the neck line which creates a curved transition from the shoulder to the neck and helps avoid straight lines which we don't want in this piece.

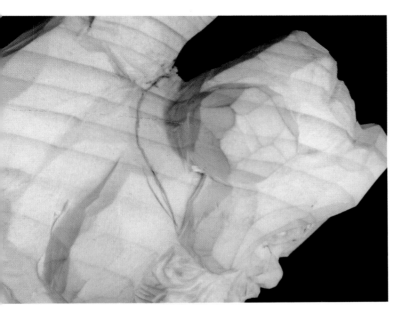

Draw in the collar.

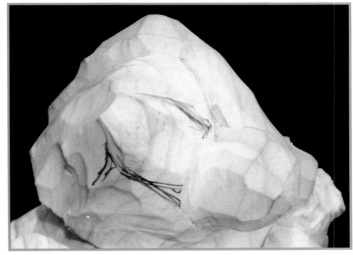

It is time to add a fold to the hat where it comes down and joins with the ball-shaped tassel. Pencil in the direction of the fold as a guide for the V tool cut to come.

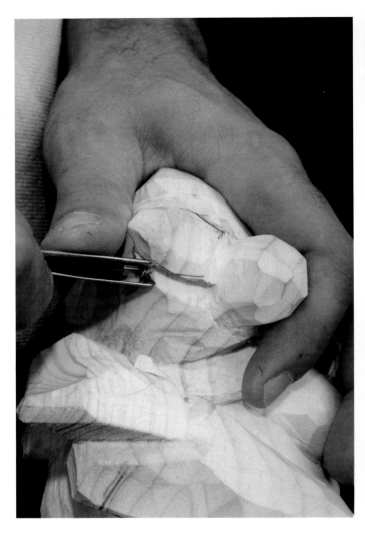

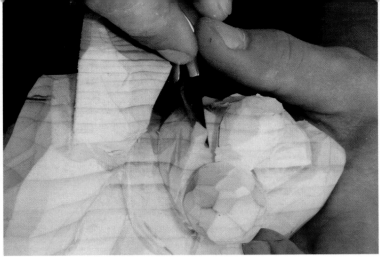

Round off the hood with the bench knife, leaving the impression that Santa's head is actually within the hood.

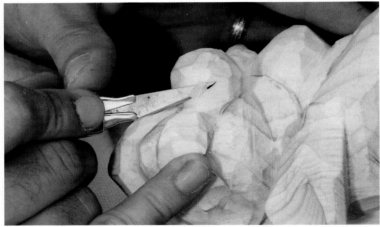

Using the #15 V tool, follow the guide lines and create the fold line from the hood to the tassel.

Round the tassel as well.

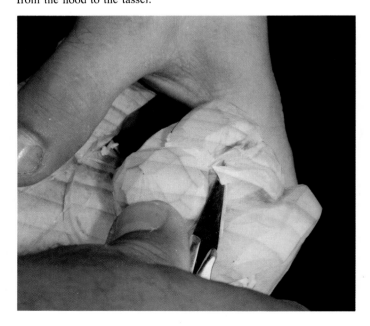

Round off the sharp edges of the fold with the bench knife.

Draw in the outline of the fish in the creel.

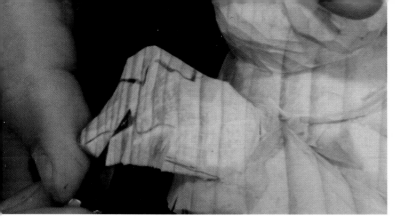

Cut in to the outline of the fish with the bench knife. Be careful as you are cutting across the grain to create this fish. The fish is slumped over in the creel.

Cut out underneath the fish to create the curve of the body and tail.

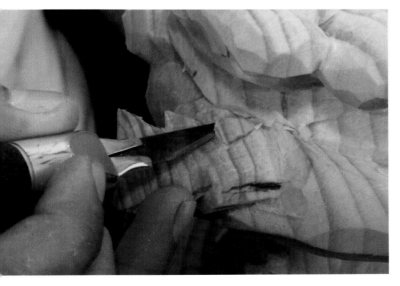

Begin to cut in the small fins. The fish's belly is up since this fish is upside down in the creel. Put in the little fins with the bench knife. Don't go too deep with each of the cuts or you will lose these small fins. When working on the fins closest the tail, support the tail from underneath to avoid breakage. When cutting in the top dorsal fin, take your time and begin cutting from the top of the fin down to where you believe the body of the fish will be. Cut back in from the body of the fish to remove the chip. Leave the fins thick for now. We will come back later to complete them after we have finished working with the fish and creel. Otherwise the fins will become too delicate and will break while we are carving other portions of the fish.

The middle fin underneath the trout is split. Make a V cut to split the fin. The smaller dorsal fin behind it is not split. Since it is difficult to carve, this fish could also be carved separately and added into the creel later.

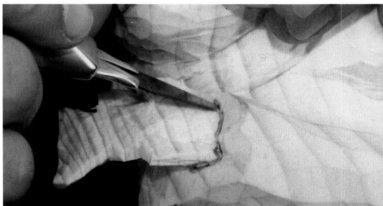

Take the knife and ride the side of the fish into the creel to create a stop cut that will allow you to make an opening in the creel, creating the illusion that the fish is stuck into the creel. Cut all the way around the fish following this pencil line.

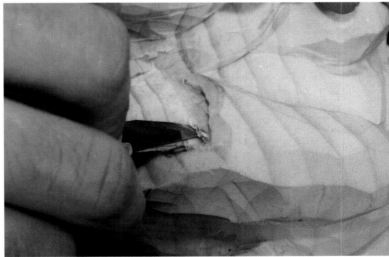

Cut back at an angle to the stop cut against the fish's side to create the creel opening. It does not have to be too deep an opening.

Now we need to square off the lip of the creel, following the penciled guide lines. I have left the lip large until now to allow me to easily carve the fish within it.

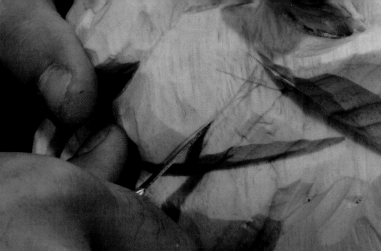

Draw in the creel strap and cut straight in along the strap lines with the bench knife to make stop cut lines. Once these stop cut lines are in, we will cut down Santa's back around them to make the straps stand out.

Trim down with the bench knife to the line of the top of the creel.

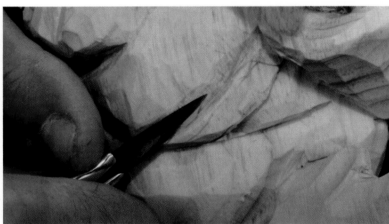

Cut back along Santa's body perpendicular to the strap stop cuts to remove excess stock from around the straps, elevating them above the back.

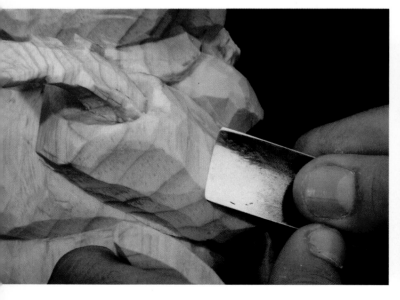

Take the #3 gouge and thin down and round off the creel somewhat so it is not quite so large.

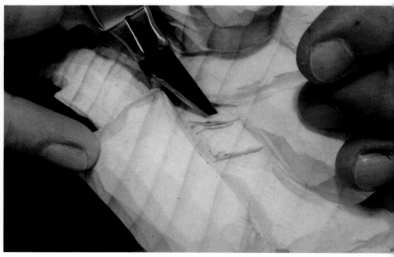

As you can see, the strap continues on around under Santa's right arm.

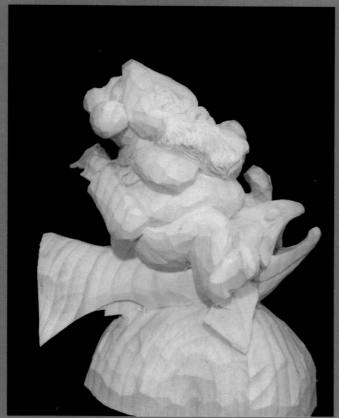
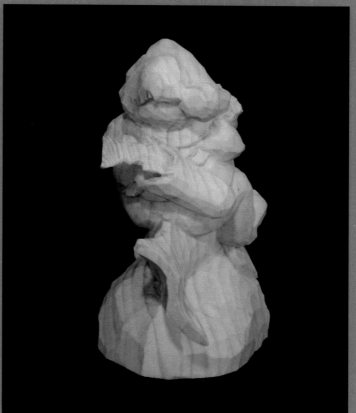

Santa and the trout are shaping up.

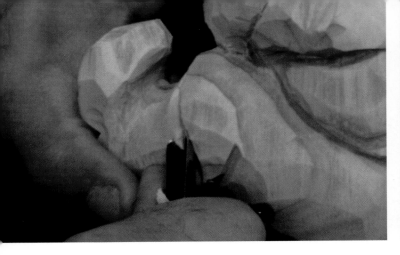

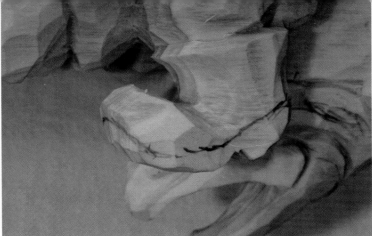

Measure the distance with a pair of calipers from the heel of the boot to the guideline at the top of the boot to make sure both are the same height. Cut out along the top of each boot with the #15 V gouge.

Draw in the sole of the boot. Make sure to bring the sole up in the front of the upraised boot to follow the curve of the foot.

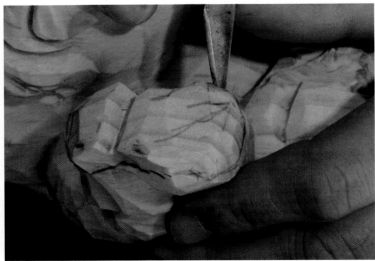

Use the bench knife to cut down the sharp edge of the pant leg and make it look as if it is tucked into the top of the boot.

Run the knife blade around the pencil line, cutting straight in to make the stop cut of the sole.

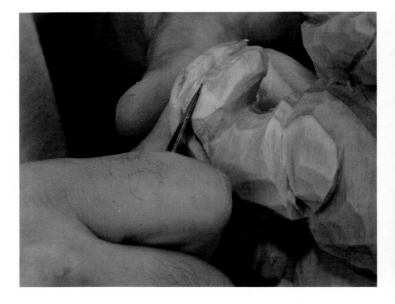

Cut in a notch for the heel; the notch should be cut straight up at the heel line and angled away ahead of it.

Round the boot down into the sole, angling back to the cut line.

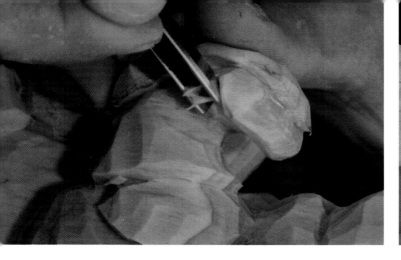

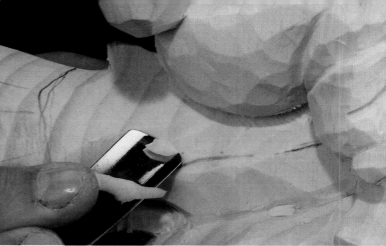

Using the #15 V tool, place a few small creases at the bends in each boot.

Thinning the fish above the line of the belly. This will give us the look of a well fed fish.

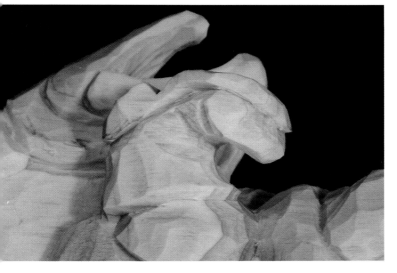

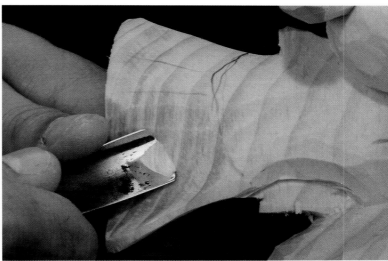

The finished boot.

While supporting the tail, thin it down from the outer edge in toward the body of the trout. Taper down the outer edge and leave the tail thicker near the fish.

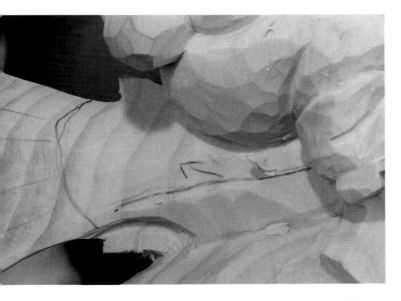

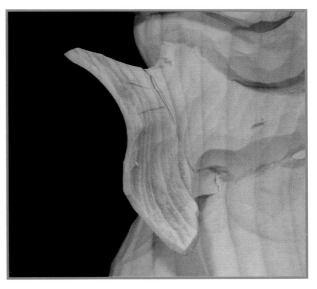

Draw in the guide lines for the belly and the tail of the trout. We are going to carve away from the top of the belly line to give the fish a rounded belly. Use the #7 gouge to thin the top.

Here is the thinned tail cross section. This is as narrow as the end of the tail needs to be.

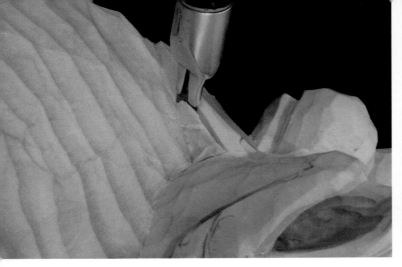

Make a very deep stop cut to undercut the leading, pectoral fins.

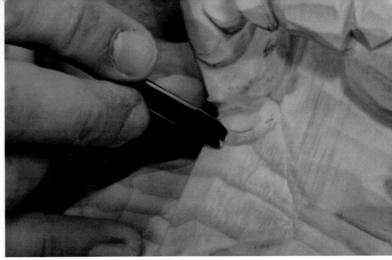

Make a semi-circle at the top of the fin where it connects with the body.

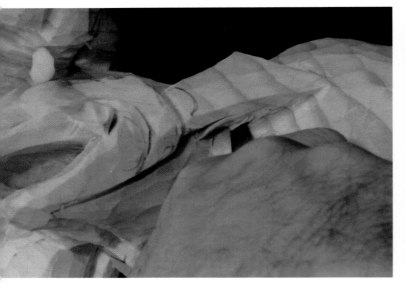

Cut back to meet the stop cut at its base and remove the chip.

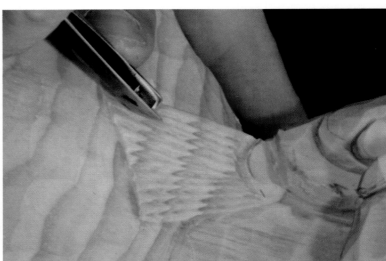

Take the V gouge and make the vertical lines in the fins. Carve in nice, close cut vertical lines in the fin with the #15 V gouge.

The undercut fins.

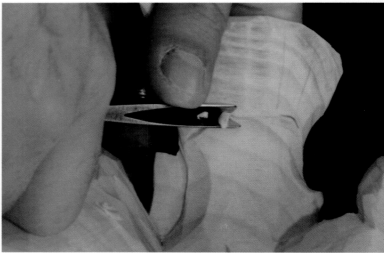

Repeat this process on the tail. Carve in the semi-circular attachment of the fish tail and body.

Carve in the close, vertical lines along the tail.

Now it is time to carve in some lines on the base to simulate water. The water is going to be trailing away from the fish in the little V wake that a fish might leave behind it. Here are the penciled guide lines to follow.

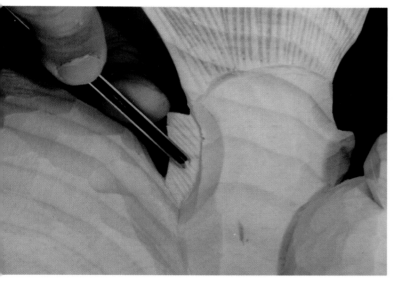

Carve in the lines at an angle on the lower back fin.

Carve in the wave lines with a bent #12 V gouge.

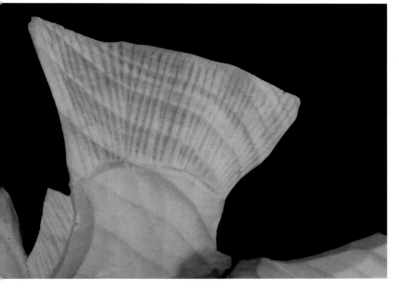

The complete tail and lower back fin.

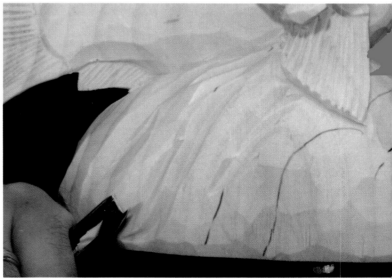

Use the flat side of the V tool to round the edges of the waves.

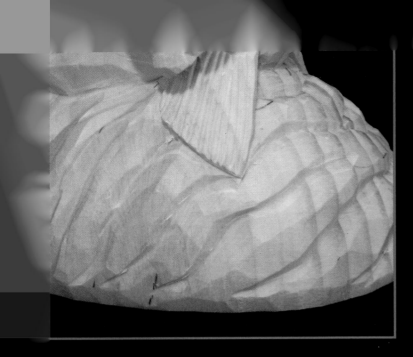

The carved waves.

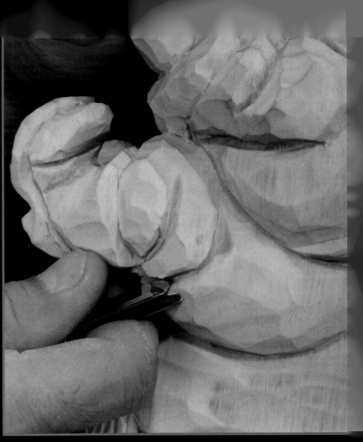

Using a #15 V tool, work around the elbows and knees and put in the creases.

Draw in several guide lines to indicate curves around the knees and elbows. You can place a couple in the coat as well if you feel like it.

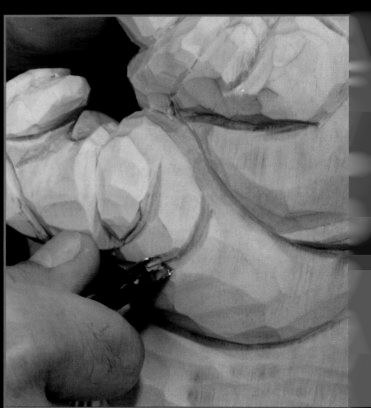

Use the flat edge of the gouge to round the sharp edges of the creases.

The fishing pole in Santa's hand is cut from 3/16" thick cherry. Cut out the pattern with the band saw.

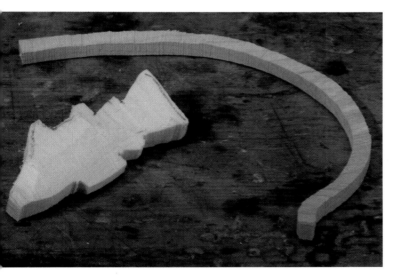

Cut out the pattern for the fishing pole and the hanging fish on the band saw.

Round down the fishing pole with the bench knife. When it is done, apply a thin coat of Minwax Natural stain to the pole.

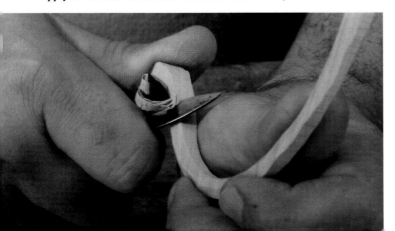

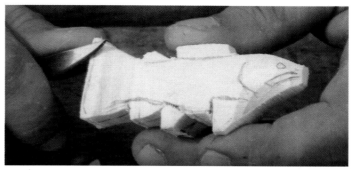

Begin rounding the small trout.

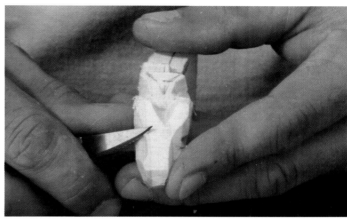

The two front fins have a split in the center (on the bottom) and the back fin is a single fin. Make a V cut in the center to split the fins. Repeat the steps above to create this smaller version of the fish Santa is riding.

Nearing completion of the small fish.

Carve in the gills, mouth, and eyes.

This is as far as we need to take this fish. We will paint in the rest of the detail.

The wood burner will also create a basket weave pattern at an angle across the surface of the creel. Burn in diagonal lines in one direction.

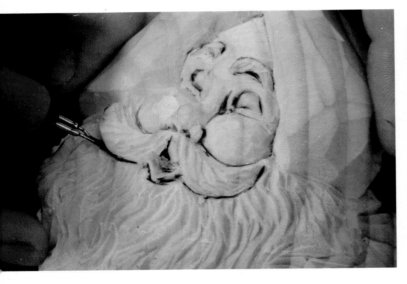

Using a wood burner, clean up any little "fuzzys" or pieces of wood that didn't cut clean on your figure. This will create a more professional, finished look. Run the burner along the hair and eyebrows, anywhere that needs some touch up. Also use the burner in areas where we will have shadows. Do not use the wood burner on a high setting. This burning step is done on all of my carvings.

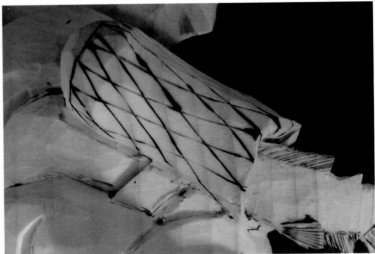

Finish the creel weave by burning diagonal lines back in the opposite direction.

Use the wood burner to create details on both the small fish in the creel and the hanging fish.

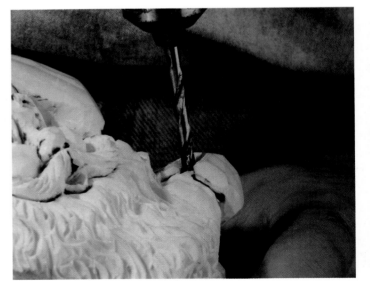

Drill a small hole in the mitten clad hands for the fishing pole.

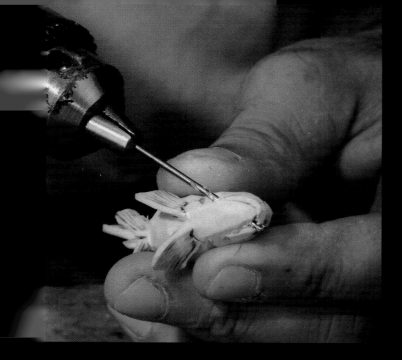

Drill a small hole through the hanging fish. A string will pass through the hole to hang this fish from the creel. Good aim is essential here.

Drill another small hole under the creel right where Santa's belt line would be. This allows the fish on the stringer to attach to the figure.

You can use either a heavy waxed thread or florist's wire for the string line. I am using florist wire because it is more durable.

The carving and wood burning are finished. The rod and stringer are in place.

Painting Santa and the Trout

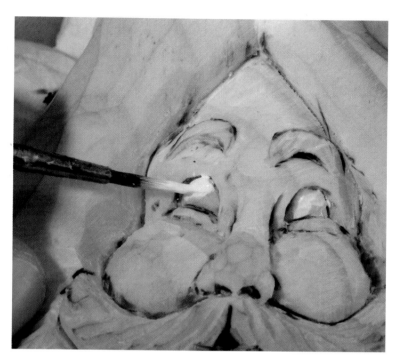

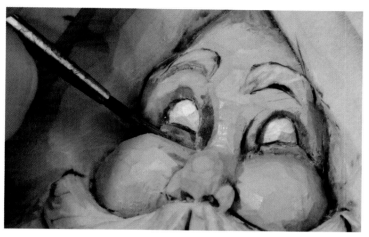

Apply a thin wash of Burnt Sienna under the eyes ...

To paint Santa we are using the following: a very soft white called Old Holland Yellow Light, flesh tint for the face, Burnt Sienna, Yellow Ocher D, Cadmium Red Pale, Raw Sienna D, Ultra Marine Blue, and Ivory Black. Mix all the colors with Minwax Natural stain to create colored stains. Beginning with the white, paint in Santa's eyes. You want to do this first so that they will be dried when you come back to paint in the irises. Apply the whites of the eyes with a #2 brush.

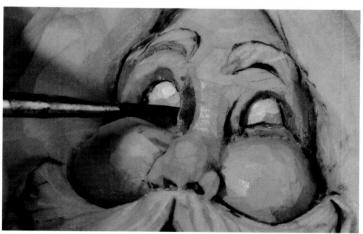

... around the insides of the eyelids...

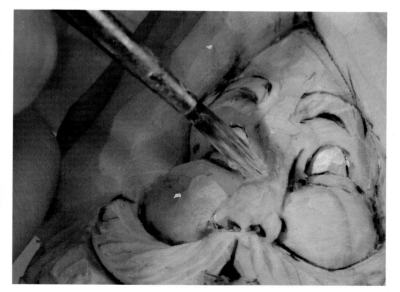

Use Flesh Tone to paint the face.

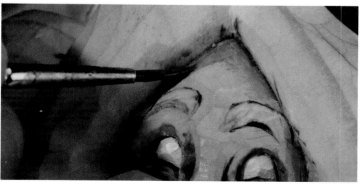

... and along the edge of the hood where the face meets the hood. All of these will be blended in.

Use Raw Sienna D at the base of the cheeks, where they meet the mustache.

... and his lower lip.

Use Light Red Pale to add red cheeks. Use this very lightly. You can always put more on later if there is not enough. Blend this color into the cheeks so you don't have big red circles on the face.

Using soft white, we will paint the beard, eyebrows, tassel, cuffs, collar, and the ruff of the hood. Again, use the color sparingly.

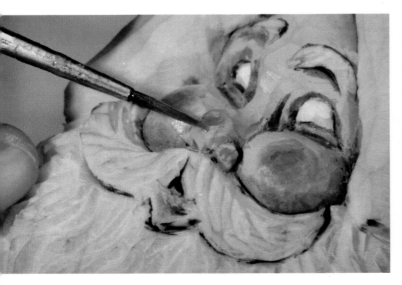

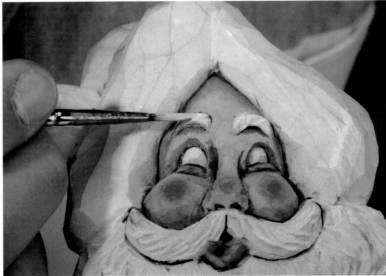

Use this Light Red Pale sparingly on the tip of Santa's nose ...

Painting the eyebrows.

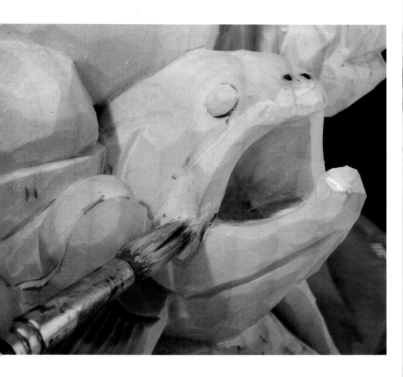

Use the white to paint in the underbelly of the trout, its flank, and around its mouth. This provides the undercoat for other colors to come.

Don't forget to add white to both small fish as well.

We are going to grey up the beard a little bit, using a dry brushing technique. Begin with a very small amount of Ultramarine Blue and Ivory Black. Dab a little paint onto the brush. Wipe most of the paint off by dragging the mix down across your paper until very little is left in the brush, spreading out the bristles as you go. Lightly flick some of this color into the beard. This produces a very nice grey.

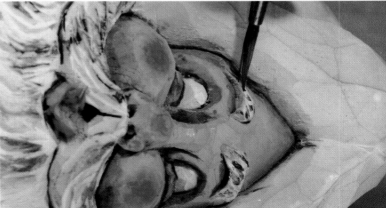

Following the same dry brushing technique, use a small #2 detail brush to add a little grey to the eyebrows. Use small, fast, short strokes to apply the color. Dance the brush across those eyebrows.

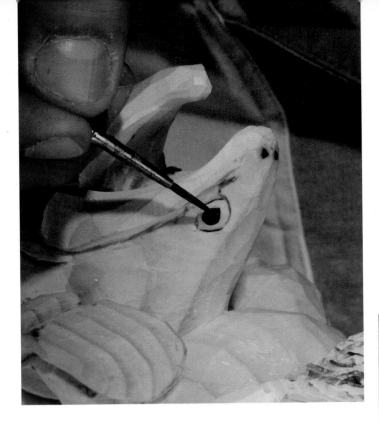

Using a little Ivory Black and the #2 detail brush, apply pupils to the fish. The pupil is a pointed egg shape.

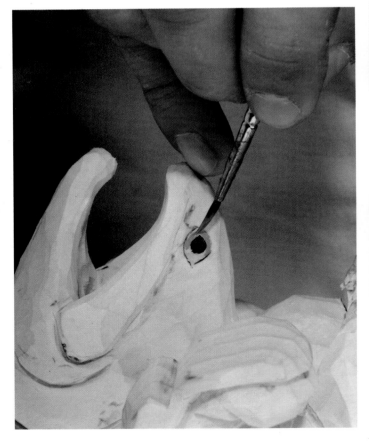

Using Orange Medium and Yellow D, create an orange-yellow for the iris of the fish's eyes. Don't forget to paint the eyes of the small fish on the stringer as well.

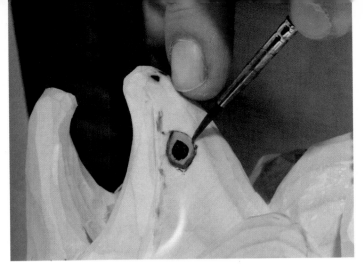

With a little Burnt Sienna, darken the outer edge of the iris of the fish.

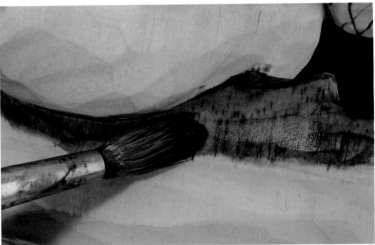

Mix Ultramarine Blue, Cadmium Yellow, and Warm Sepia (Chocolate Brown) to produce the color for the top half of the fish. Paint each fish with this dark olive green color. Remember to apply this as a light wash. Begin applying this to the back and blend it down the sides.

Applying the olive green to the stringer fish.

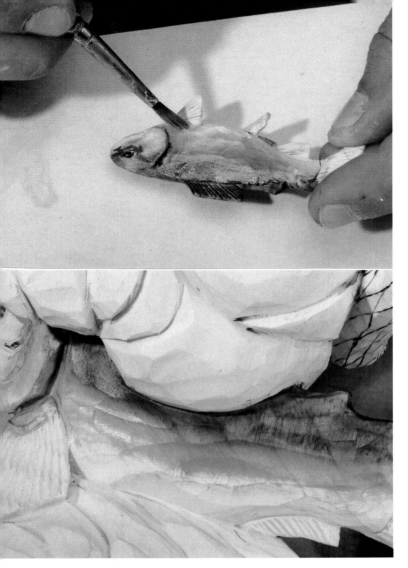

Using a very small amount of the remaining brown and olive green paints, tone down the white of the jaw line and lower jaw.

Use Yellow Ocher D mixed with just a touch of Orange to create a mustard yellow to be used on the middle side of the fish. Once this color has been applied, all three colors will be blended (the olive green, Yellow Ocher D and white) together. Remember to paint all three fish at once so you will not have to go back and try to recreate these colors later. These three color bands duplicate an iridescent effect on the scales of a fish.

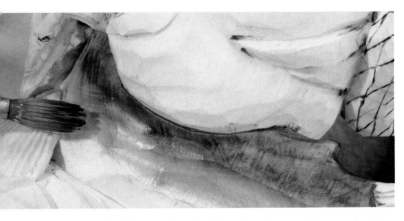

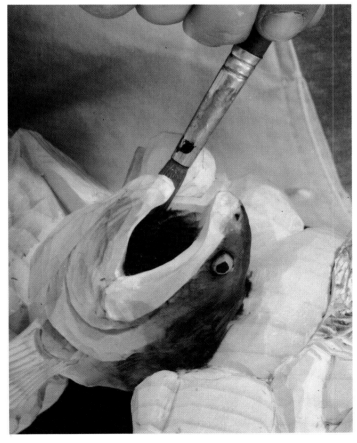

Spread out the bristles of the brush by dragging the olive green paint out. Using a very small amount of paint, drag quickly across the side of the fish to create a scaled effect. This works well provided your paint is not to watery.

Using a little bit of black, darken the mouth and blend it around the inside edges with the white from the jaws.

Use Raw Sienna to paint the creel and the strap. It is a warm color that works well with the fish.

Mix a little Burnt Sienna and Yellow Ocher to create a brown color and paint the fins and the tail.

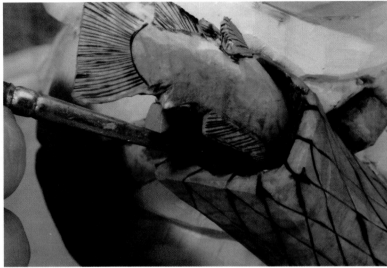

Use Warm Sepia to create a dark shadow inside the creel around the fish ...

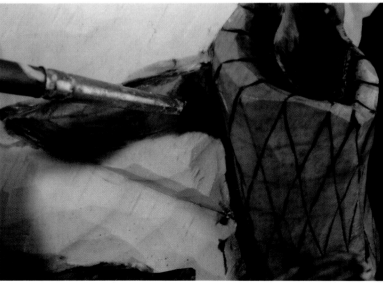

Blend a little Raw Umber into the tail and fins as well. These blends help tie the fish together. T'.e amount of blending you do is up to you. I prefer to blend a lot. Fish are fun to play with that way. Be creative.

... and in other areas of shadow as well.

The time has come to put in spots. Mix white, black, ultramarine blue, and raw umber to create a medium slate grey color. This is the background color of the spots. We don't want the spots to be too bright or to be to heavily applied as we don't need any big buildup of paint here. We are going to be adding colors on top of many of these spots. Additionally, the dots should not be uniform in intensity or evenly spaced. These spots appear on the top and flanks of this brown trout.

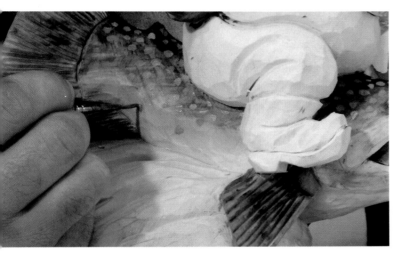

The spotted side.

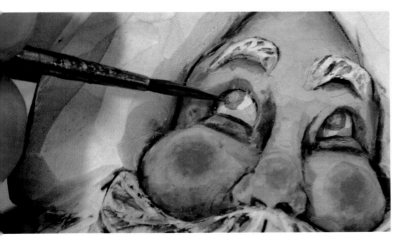

Mix white with ultramarine blue to create Santa's iris. Leave the centers of the irises lighter and the outer edges darker.

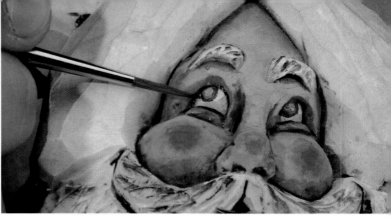

Add a dark ring of ultramarine blue to the outer edge of each iris. This creates very striking blue eyes.

Using Warm Sepia, make a very light wash. Take the paint on to your large brush and touch it to the end of the tail where it joins the body. The paint will run down the troughs of the tail bones to highlight the ridges in the tail. Repeat this process on the pectoral fins.

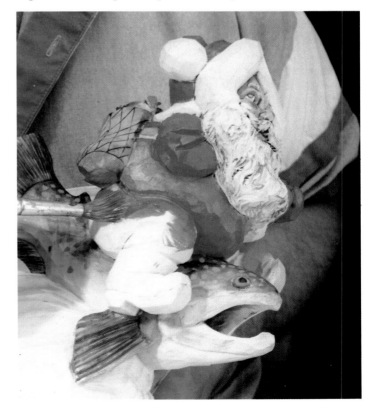

Use Cadmium Red D to paint Santa's suit, hat, gloves, mittens, and pants.

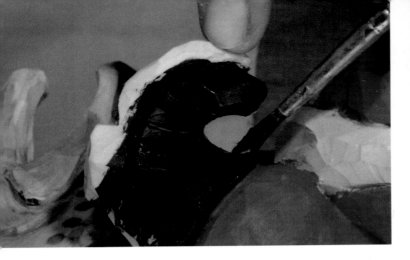

Mix Ivory Black with a little white to create a smokey blackish-grey for Santa's boots. Don't paint the soles of the boots yet.

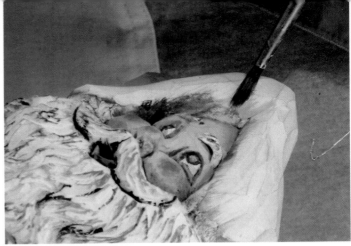

Use Raw Umber to put a little shadow in the hood.

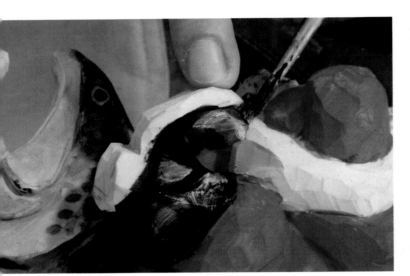

Add a little white highlight to the boots.

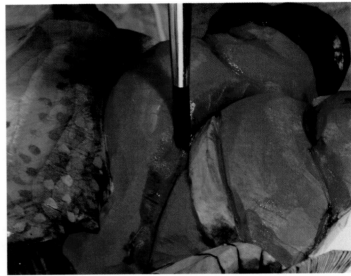

Ultramarine blue will make shadows in the creases in Santa's suit, pants, and around his mittens. This is applied in a very thin wash. Blue is a very strong color and easily overused.

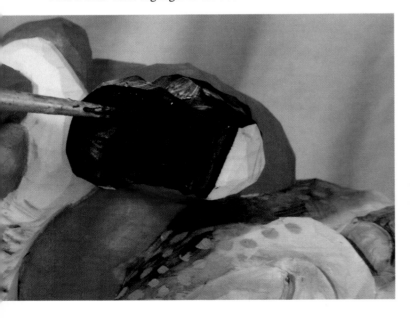

Paint the soles of the boots pure black.

Use a larger brush dipped in Minwax to blend the blue shadow out into the suit. This will create an uneven coloration which give nice gradations around the suit itself.

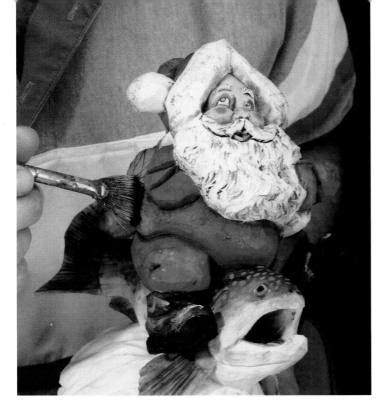

You can also place a few tiny black dots off by themselves wherever you think they would look best.

Take a fan blender brush and dab it in black paint which has not been thinned in Minwax (making sure the paint is only on the tips of the fan). Punch the palette with the brush until very little paint is left on the tips of the bristles and then stipple the coat with what's left. This will give the coat a velvet texture. Dab it all around until you have a multitude of tiny black dots. Stipple the coat, hood, tassel ... all parts of Santa's clothing except for his boots. After the stippled black is completely dry, go back and repeat the stippling process in red on the clothing and white on the white fur trim.

Continuing with the mix of Van Dyke Brown, Black, and Ultramarine Blue, place small dots on the tail and the fins.

Mix Van Dyke Brown, Black, and a touch of Ultramarine Blue to make the centers of the grey spots on the fish. Thin the mixture down with Minwax Natural and apply. When applying black dots, leave an occasional grey background dot open. Brown trout have red centers in some of the spots. These occur randomly.

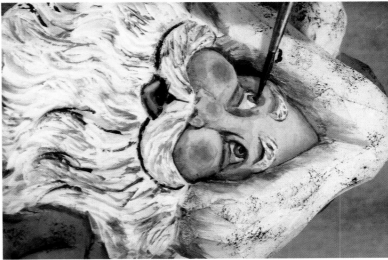

Continuing with the mix of Van Dyke Brown, Black, and Ultramarine Blue, add pupils to the centers of Santa's eyes with a #2 brush.

With Cadmium Red D, apply red dots to the grey spots left open earlier. Don't forget the little fish.

Now that the black stippling is dry, mix Schevenings Red Pale with Orange and use the fan blender again to stipple on the areas where highlights would be found on Santa's clothes. Only use this on the highlights.

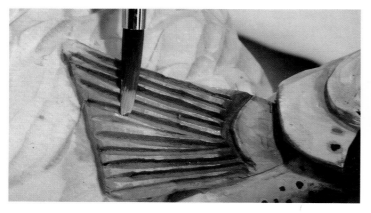

Put a little straight Cadmium Yellow on the brush and swipe perpendicularly across the tops of the fins to add highlights.

Use a little white and grey to put in a small wisp of hair curling out from under the hood.

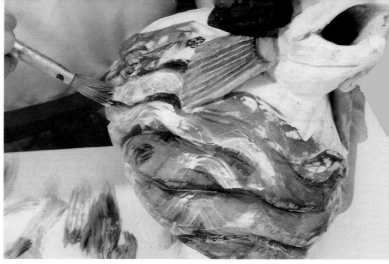

Use Ultramarine Blue, Yellow, and Black ... anything on the palette except red, and apply across the base to create the color of the sea. Use your imagination here. Apply colors in bold, undulating strokes, generally following your cut waves. Do some dry brushing as well. Create the look of a turbulent sea.

Use a little Black mixed with Minwax Natural to darken the wave troughs.

Using the #2 brush, apply white highlights in the trout's eyes. Make sure they both fall in the same spot in each eye.

Antiquing Santa and the Trout

Before applying an antiquing mixture, the carving must dry for a day or two. Prior to antiquing a figure, I spray it with a thin coat Deft Semi-Gloss Clear Wood Finish.

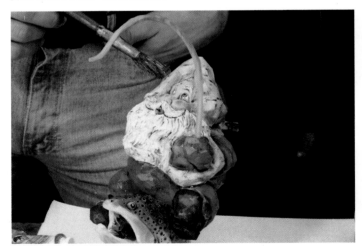

Once the carving is dry, make a very thin wash of Burnt Umber and Minwax (you can also use Raw Umber if you want a lighter finish), take a very wide brush (we're not looking for consistency throughout, just to blend the colors and remove any starkness from the piece), and apply. You can wipe some of this mix away with a cloth if you wish. I like to apply the coat a little heavier in the beard to show texture and lighter in the face. Everywhere else, I just let it go where it will. This is fun after all the hard work. Enjoy!

Notice the difference in the coated ruff of the hood and the uncoated beard. The antiquing mix has been applied lightly to the face.

Now the coating has been heavily applied in the beard.

Add pure white highlights to the eyes, a little off center from the pupil. The small brush you use should have only a tiny amount of paint on its tip. Lightly touch the brush to the eyes.

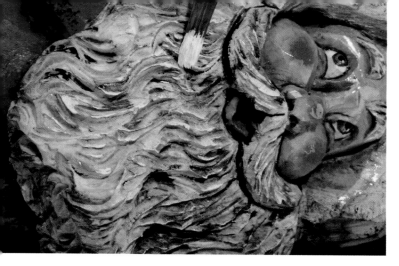

Dry brush the beard with pure white paint. Just brushing the bristles perpendicularly across the beard and mustache will pick up the highlights in white. Use your own judgement as to how much highlighting to do.

Add a little white highlight to the fish's mouth and to the wave crests.

Add highlights to the eye of the little fish on the stringer as well.

Using a pair of plier, push a small pin (cut in half so as not to be too long) into the corner of the trout's mouth.

Using the blender brush, dry brush a little pure white on the white fur areas and the tassel. This will liven up the piece.

Make a slip knot in the thread "fishing line," attach it to the pin, push the pin flat into the trout's mouth, cut off the excess and tie the other end of the fishing line to the end of the pole. A little glue applied to both ends of the thread will keep it from coming untied. Use a very small amount of glue so that it is not obvious. You can paint over the head of the pin when you are through if you wish. Spray a little Deft to you fingers and coat the line with it to get rid of the "fuzzys."

The finished project. Congratulations!

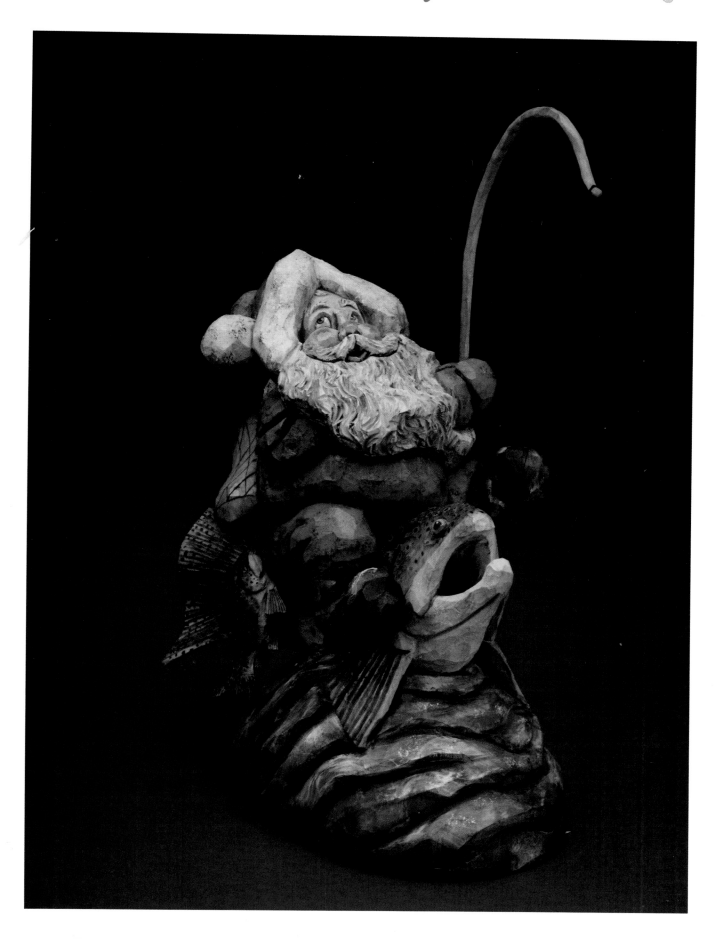

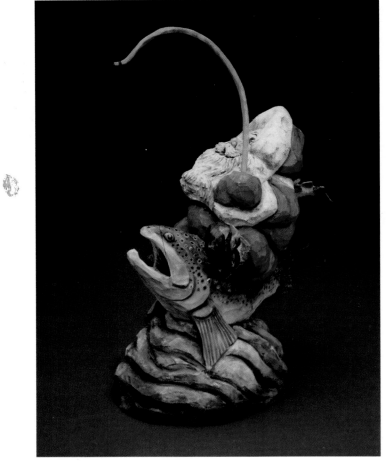

Hand is carved open to accept the
Christmas Dove

4" wide

Grain Direction

Pattern reduced to 58% of original size.

Mrs. Claus

Pattern reduced to 58% of original size.

Last Package

Pattern reduced to 58% of original size.

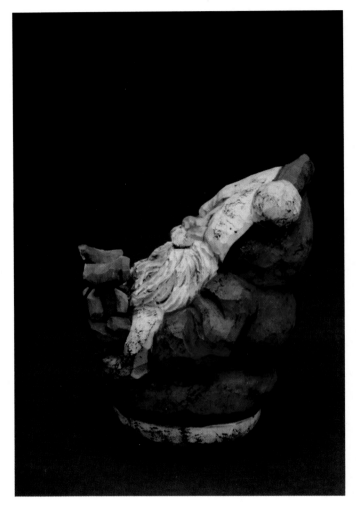

Chef Santa:

Pattern reduced to 58% of original size.

Pattern reduced to 58% of original size.

Pattern reduced to 58% of original size.

Pattern reduced to 58% of original size.

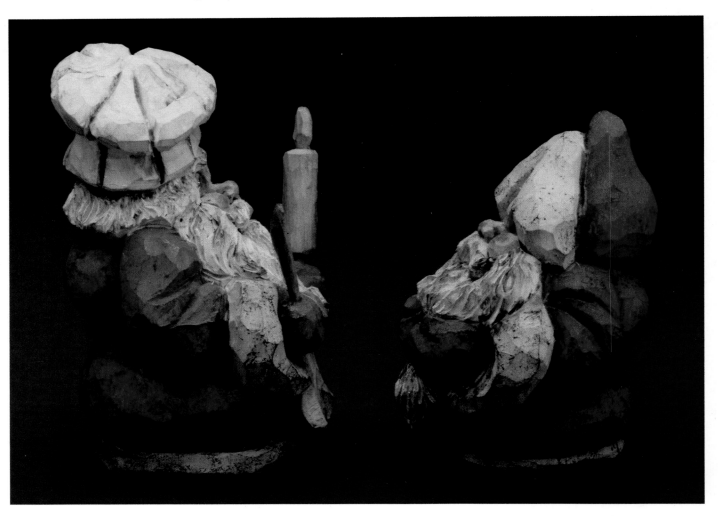

Other Books by David Sabol

Text written with and photography by Jeffrey B. Snyder

Carving Noah's Ark: Mrs. Noah & Friends, The Animals of North America

Traditional carving and realistic painting applied to a timeless subject: Noah's Ark. Step-by-step techniques for carving Noah's wife or one of several animals native to North America. Patterns include: Mrs. Noah, two turkeys, pumas, rabbits, foxes, raccoons, skunks, and opossums.

Size:8 1/2" x 11"   64 pages
250 color photos   Patterns for 18 figures
ISBN: 0-88740-731-5   soft cover $12.95

Carving Noah's Ark: Monkeys and Apes

Monkeys and apes have come aboard Noah's ark to enliven the ship, keeping Noah and his crew on their toes. Monkeys swing from the rafters and hoot from the bow. Apes cuddle, roar and lounge about the deck. All are animated with detailed expressions and gestures which David Sabol uses to bring his carvings to life. David takes the reader through every step in the transformation of a block of pine into a monkey or ape with enjoyable, straight-forward directions accompanied by clear color photographs. The traditional carving techniques he employs are explained in detail. Wood burning and oil staining bring each carving to life. With the mastery of these traditional techniques, the entire animal kingdom is yours to carve and add to the passenger list of your very own ark.

Size: 8 1/2" x 11"   64 pages
Over 270 color photographs   17 patterns
ISBN: 0-88740-971-7   soft cover $12.95

Carving Noah's Ark; Noah and Friends With the Animals of Africa

Now you can populate your own ark with sprightly wooden animals from Africa, two by two. Noah himself will be there to supervise. David Sabol brings this best-known nautical odyssey to life with a series of vividly carved and painted animal and biblical characters.

David instructs his readers in the use of traditional carving and realistic painting techniques which give his carvings a distinctive design, personality, and charm all their own. A combination of clear explanation and color photos makes each stage of the process a pleasure.   64 pages
Size: 8 ½" x 11"   272   color photos   24 Patterns
                                            soft cover $12.95
                              ISBN: 0-88740-779-X